HOW TO EAT FIRE AND WHY

HOW TO EAT FIRE AND WHY

MITCH CAVE

Rabbit. | *Poets Series*

Rabbit Poetry Journal would like to acknowledge the people of the Woi wurrung and Boon wurrung language groups of the eastern Kulin Nations on whose unceded lands this book was created, designed, produced, printed and distributed. We respectfully acknowledge their Ancestors and Elders, past and emerging.

Published by Rabbit Poetry Journal
as part of the Rabbit Poets Series
www.rabbitpoetry.com

Series editor: Jessica L. Wilkinson
Assistant editor: Renee Cahill
Cover image: Christopher Zanko, *Unanderra Swan Garden*, 2021 acrylic on wood relief carving 79 x 77cm
Typesetting, layout and cover design: Christopher Black

Printed in Australia by Print Strategy Management
Mitch Cave, *how to eat fire and why*, Rabbit Poets Series, No. 16
ISBN: 978-0-6453366-3-4

Photo credit: Connor Smith

Mitch Cave grew up in Noosa Heads, Queensland, and is a writer and performer currently based in Brisbane. His work has appeared in literary journals nationally as well as internationally. He works in the disability sector and has English, German, Māori, Ukrainian and Polish family heritage.

contents

I lost everything in a house fire when I was 19 years old, including all of the poems I'd ever written, a loss that sparked the idea for this collection. These poems are not only acts of remembering and recovery; together, they shape a mind map of endurance, grief, courage, relationships, destruction and healing.

air

how i got home from noosa last night

our hands are bound
by a neon dawn
no one will be swallowed
by its glow
saliva
yellow perhaps
though we never quite decided
on a vacancy
we will next inhabit
and so we wait
until constellations
overlap our mouths
hushed in frog patience
waiting for someone else's sky
to break the news of rain
she has turned towards me
salient
her absent face
reminds me of the peculiarities
found in broken eggs
and then her flesh
reminds me of burning carpet
but between
heavy eyelids and
summers with rain music
our gentle pasts
begin to illuminate themselves
intertwine
as worms arrive beneath
our feet
begin to crack pavements
silence
my hair smiles
morphing into the paper of
a novel i have never read
beside me
the smoke of a forgotten bird

offers me a lift home
yes
pulls me inside myself
and i levitate
think about how
the labyrinths warned
i will begin decomposing
moments before the sky
presents itself
voodoo trees
eclipse

uber ride or, the circumnavigation of jasper blue moon

jasper who's strutting down
ocean street maroochydore
jasper who's getting in the
car mouth blatantly shut how
delicate are his hands cupped
collecting wind sand falls onto
the car floor but that's showbiz
baby sacrificial goat have
you got the key this is
lifeblood speaking how may i
help you ring ring no answering
machine body to body he keeps
his wits about him tongue and
alive this is how he was born
gotta go gotta get going gotta
not a good look to jaywalk he
decides to cross just up the road
from the cop shop goon bag is
swishing in his backpack gotta
go gotta get going gotta fox
runs alongside him on the
footpath brisk terrain to touch
new kneecap new apartment he
wears a new body so his old one
doesn't get damaged anymore he
who won't be stagnant lying in a
bed of dandelions he who wears
the blue moon jeans without
being asked to he whom i
adore and nevertheless
despise like rainfall

splendid is the sun orbiting around you

closing stone you
and me in a marcoola
apartment complex

cerulean dreaming
in the soft night
air you nurse a fever
          pale water
          rushing to your head

of course there are
rules that we follow

hold raw flesh in one hand and
signal small fires to burn
around my body

i peruse
    the dense grass
          that keeps me hidden from the others

blood stain
thickens in the carpet

when i am not blind i
                      notice that your body is
hurricane across ground
                      your legs twisted into
shape of crossbow hallway
                      bends with your echo

i meet your mother in the morning
if you stare long enough
her skin will shade into
                   dark wine

the bedroom window is starless
i hear your whispers but get you
to verify your identity through each
cup of chai smashed across the floor

you are swollen in my arms
to keep you there
i think of the indigo
that wakes inside of you

winds
blowing

at your disposal

last night i heard
your voice the sound
is all i can remember i
can hear it again i am
coughing up jam
*
there are snakes
folded up inside
my mouth hissing
*
there is a wine glass
embedded in my cranium
it is beautiful life is so beautiful
and we communicate—
*
—if poets were as famous as rappers
the world would be
a very scary place
*
i have seen you wrap bodies
in plastic once you are done
with them
ask me: will
i do the same or
should i save the environment
*
gently he edges closer to
me closer in wind gust and
we shall become immortal
*
you have decided i will not
wear clothing anymore my
body is simply too ugly
to be hidden
*

i am a cactus
more of a prick
than you'd think
*
you're a bougainvillea
also a prick but still
pretty some would say
*
life is still
so beautiful

fuckboy

there are many misinterpretations in this
bedroom such as how the demon that knocks
on the window is in fact a tree branch and if you

were an animal you'd be a gentle lorikeet but
you did just trip over an oscillating fan so

tilted on the wall insert your
body inside a cheese grater and

once you are shredded illumine my bad luck
on the flokati rug i too can transform into a

bird if that's what you really want me to do my
wings expand and the weather rotates and i

start holding my breath as one door opens on us so
you carefully select flower petals off the ground and

eat them i am bored now and this means in
my head i am baking cupcakes again i guess

my attention span is nearly as short as you
are lonely without your fangs and it shows

still you are a goblin so i cannot remember
where i placed my underwear
and now this is awkward

car crash

bunny ears baby get in go
get your paws off me blood
on your shirt on the wheel on
your eye press together to
combine every bruise of
time into one small
minute or play the
guitar until you

calm
fall
lay

down into town in your new
automobile seat reclined smooth
drive in the latex of your forbidden

chariot
ring
doves

flocking to the burial ground and tyre
bursts brace yourself lamborghini slices
into danger bending as if to welcome ghost
gum of your own skin undulating upon mine
and then your breathing will slow and i will
make sounds with my lungs until you
slowly rise and then find your
own way out the
dark way

cold feet

absolve and you've
become an aquarium
inspired i've become such a
burden my wings are still there
but that's about it so here we
are again waiting for the flares
to pass i still remember that
time you taught me how
to form a symphony with
my opened mouth how
still everything becomes
around us then eventually
crooked i just
don't think i can keep
doing things like this i'm
sorry to have to tell you but
whatever's crawled up inside of
me well i guess it's become truly fucking
pluto circumference exponential are
you there that was
the letterbox this time

come dine with me

psychic batteries and
nocturnal vegetables
follow me to the oven
i crave tip toe tip toe
the crisp of purple
nightfall and desk
fan blowing on the
postponed wine you
will find me underneath
the table for the rest of
the evening

party pooper

i don't do very well at parties because
i am afraid because i am
a bag of flesh dispersed
across the floor or i am made
out of harp strings and you'll
call me by my first name and
reminisce about how many
times i used to fill up my cup
but this shouldn't harm you
so we will speak until time
passes through our windpipes
and the morning begins to rise
around us pausing to crystallise
in the empty streets while we
consider redeveloping the shape
of our skeletons upstairs and i
will flower my skin lilac and you'll
shout words at me and you'll sever my
head and leave it on lucy's front doorstep
and part of me thinks that this is the only
truth there is left to be considered so we just
leave we are running we are disappearing we
are running again and that is the last time
i think we will ever speak so i deal
with this on my own terms call
a cab and arrive home with
glass in my pocket

when i tell you to run, you must run

remnants of barbed wire will
clarify our wide tongues we
can both be glorious and still
vanish into each other watch
and i will demonstrate not
during any rush hour
my wingspan

earth

observations from the balcony, barmore street

dandelion crouches into
a ball nursing nostril quiet
as red slides down the centre
of his cracked arrow mouth
*
soft music draws
ink from the ears or
hear the mortifying comfort
of another's flesh beside you
*
unscrews with
claws smearing into jar
of caviar lick jelly of carcass
black fish rotten doorframe
*
deck chair exposes wall milk
and then yellow plants are
corrupted by tree dust
it's all so sad now
*
washing dangles and they
study their hands decide
to smile one last
time azure nebula
*
hand left to soak in dish water
welcomed by cyclonic
air carried from harbours of
seafood calculus it's about time
*
snails gather in the corner to
create a new lullaby one that is
happy to accommodate
silent aggressions
*
rust but make it
fashion   does not cater for people like
me   the mermaid clock
                        turns

tamara or, carry me like sunlight

ornamented as in dogs
are gathering about
her body ferns shield
the light emanating
from her mouth you can
see them at the close of day
things that orbit around
her and which she
has absorbed to pull
herself free she
watches a toadstool
open its mouth and whisper
about a merry-go-round
still she becomes fairy
during quake or treefall
collects the coat dangling
from the clothesline and
begins to dance she has seen
things no other fairy has
seen and yet flowers bend
toward her steps she is
running with the dogs and
no she does not have to
look back

babcia’s ghost helps me gain weight

babcia appears
in the mirror her skin
less stretched lavender
fronds in her hair and
she smiles frequently
whispers your recovery is
soft creeping like a ghoul
around the linen cupboard
babcia whispers you know
i am a ribbon around
you and honeybees
are decorated down your
oesophagus patiently i have
not been stung in almost
a decade babcia says
i’m becoming gaunt again
prepares a meal with sage and
cabbage watches my jaw gobble
what is left of the bowl thinned
the way i used to be now i am
full babcia leaves
and i am still here

piece of cake

the deer are illuminated upon
the hillside smoulders we
carry on home as it gets
dark and your veins are
bluer than i remember i've
entered this room and of
course there are burial
fruits and then by my
side you have been
swallowing cake again
this is the way it should
be like this i
eat with your hands

hail storm on halloween

clOuds fOrm green
abOve us fOrtitude
valley get intO car heavy
with fall On rOad with
yOu with me with eye Of
the stOrm nOt befOre
sky nOw drOps Off
ice yOur hand On my
thigh we can Only be
safe take the Other
turn Off Or every
bead Of hail that
ejects frOm clOud
break echOes upOn
dent rOOf glare
Of ether hOw
cOnvenient and
nOw sheltering

panic room at a party

dO yOu reCognISe wHaT mY facE
loOks liKe wheN i OpeN tHE dooR
tO yOur SWollEN boDy yOur skIn
tuRns inTo waTer On TuEsDaYs
appEars liKe sMall MoUnTaInS
surrOundinG uS aNd yoUr cOrAl
moUth oPeNs beCoMes a tuNNel
oF trEEs sPreaDinG aParT inTo
a rEvIsIoN oF mOOnFLOWers
reSTiNG agAinst yoUr FairY liGhT
sKull wOn'T eVen fEEL liKe tHiS
forEVeR beCauSe tHis iS pAniC tHiS
iS thE rOoM iN wHiCh WE eNtEr tO
DIscarD tHe viOliN strIng bOdy iNtO
hOt lAvA thIS iS hOw yOung wE reAllY
aRe iN thE discOursE oF sMalL bErrIeS
pLaCeD arounD ouR dIscO bAll LiMbS
thiS is tReMbLiNg wItHoUt aNy rulES thiS
iS waTchInG aS iF yOu wIll nOt bE eNteR
tAmEd By mY beniGn aLLocatIon
oF sToP!
dRoP!
aNd! RoLL

the garden's absolution

palm frond:
would you look at that: the earth is flamed with light now. the deck chair is neon green. i wish you could be here to see it. your limbs have been discarded. you missed the cremation. i'm sorry it had to be that way.

flower:
there is an unpeeled orange in my palm. its texture makes me crave the feeling of iron deficiency running down my chin. i am several years older than i look and my dietary needs are not your own. do not run from me this time, i mean you no harm.

palm frond:
who stole the lasagne? i have eyes in the back of my head. i watched you pinch at woolies. who am i to deny you of your discrepancy? you're free to go.

flower:
you are not who you think you are. the road you arrived here on is decorated with collapsed trees. perhaps they are being farmed for sap the way i farm you for your secrets. you must not swallow the nectar anymore.

palm frond:
if i see you running from the others, i will have to join them. we've all travelled a distance to reach this point. it's time to choose.

flower:
i have never haunted anyone, i only wish to be forgiven. i will dance around your body with glowing arms. i will swallow fire and leave out sugar water for the bees. tell me what i have to do.

palm frond:
no one is going to make it out of here alive, that's a given.

hypnosis for weathered bodies

                    wasp omen and
gust now leaving
                    moth of the mouth
you go still under
                    the heaviness of night
clifftop and patient you
                    are monsoon an arrow
loosened upon a bow was
                    not half asleep yet you
still hunger for a crow
                    dawn click back
into place bone
                    by bone

homebody

wake up leaf dream

i have made the

bed leave when day

turns blue berry left

in bowl you're still

like flower resting in

vase pour coffee to

warm up hands and

this is home you

are home right now

harvest of fruit

i am hungry again and so i think of you as a pineapple. fancied, beginning again as i slice the flesh. my hands will tremble from time to time but that's just life and i know i am not afraid anymore. if the men come for us i will just pin them down on their backs and drink their blood. things are simpler when you are a swan. i was once. do not ignore me when i say it's time to leave our bodies; the trees have blown in my direction. his death strangles you and you weep like candles do and i will always forgive you for this. the snow falls early in parts of this country. i break things. i will always be sorry.

water

venus as a boy in a dream

after the song by björk

his body washes up
on the shoreline
sea foam draped
around his thighs
and so i drag him
across the sand
soft as i conjure
his moonlit neglect
harnessing what is
left of his gemstone
skin two pretty fins
shake and glow and
carry his weight as
shark tails spread
across the shoreline
welcomed in cloud
he is heavy rain in
my drenched bone
under and immortal
his eye sockets now
somewhat closed over
without daybreak he
will never appear again

pond water

lying in a body of water
saturday around me

algae meridians
attached to my delicate flesh

my legs spread across
the breadth of a deserted lily pad

i will sometimes allow men
to touch my body

allow their hands
to wrap around my throat

indefinitely
they will pull me underwater

release my skull
chin glowing with glue water

and after i gasp for air drag
me by my hair to the shoreline

my hands
bound with seagrass

if i scream they
will place pieces of quartz

underneath my tongue
to disfigure me

the men leave eventually
and now i am stillness

silence
venus flytrap on my left

soil
in my berry skin

and life is so beautiful
here uncollected beside

the ruins of a mutilated dragonfly
bobbing atop the shoreline

self-care

i am not without
the smooth polish of a vessel
my bathtub of surf swirling
with dolphins seaweed
grows inside my
mouth there is
a cure swallow
the wound
come undone

hilton esplanade, tewantin

anticipated knock
of the boat tides
pulling in around you

wash up on the shoreline
your mouth damp with salt
dribbling into mangrove

see i was raised
like a wishbone
always quieted

i remove the river
from my eyes so i
can see you better

swarm of beetles
mobilising into thick
clustered tree stumps

they too feed the
mouth kept unwatered
in the bathroom sink

the pelicans have left us
to discard wedding rings
on a monday afternoon

hour of brick wall bruise
imprinted across cheekbones
as sun vanishes into sand shadow

houseboats kept
upright and hindered
with dawn undiscovered

the fish have come home
my mouth becomes
their swimming pool

everything is purple
and you are no
longer standing

palm spreads open
you wake inside
a dog's body

like tsunami
we're all born
to make decisions

think of this now as i
drift off to my riverbed
state of piranha-fearing

slush puppie machine

straw dance one
miss i sip slush
water leave the
tap running away
from you take a
left down monarchy
street abandon the tiger
teeth glistening in the
swimming pool baby
we don't need that
on our conscience

the ocean is looking at us

i told you once when you
speak your voice sounds
like small pebbles falling
out of your mouth you
untie yourself from my
pinky finger there you
are gliding under
water i can be a
dark ocean law
abiding citizen the
waves have come to
a halt did you
know that already

dreamscape: tropic of capricorn

mosquitoed telephones ring
around my mossy disconnect
or violet lips corroded into
judgements and poor eyesight
mumbling along a wave crest
with whale i am forming an
army helicopters from ear to
ear you don't see me
coming you
are parts inside of me that
need to be diagnosed or
you are soft like nightfall
there will always be
mountains nearby and blood
will always make me shiver
swallowing watermelon seeds
my neon thumb shall not
press into your temple
anymore

house of perpetuating water

during the wintertime we smile less
slice paper into shapes with blades

to keep you happy i lick
the wounds on your hands

watch you levitate most nights
as i wait beside the shoreline

in the garden you carry birds behind
your back as if i would not notice

the meadow saturates with dew and i
hold onto you through the clearing fog

your fingers cross into mine
and i cannot see your eyes anymore

we are cindered neglect and shadowed
small beneath clouds that nurse vapour

then watch as i congeal into the cobalt
dustpan of someone you once loved

moon pulling tidewaters i
returned distant that year

carried the weight
until i could not

supermoon king tides, noosa heads

i'm dreaming of water again
the world is ending
*
supermoon king
tides welcome i
am enlightened
on your silver
buttered shores
*
you told me you were born
inside a quilt of sea and
i did not believe you
*
i used to wake
up early observe you
escorting the froth traffic
with the muscles in your arms
*
blades of light slash
across your back
make you dive
deeper small fish
greet you smile
and say hello
*
sapphire wave
smooth in the underflow
that drags my body across the
surface and onto a cloak of sand
*
we take shelter inside
a cave bleeding
with graffiti we
must not bow to
turtles with no shells
*

you rest neatly inside
the shade of your cheeks
your amethyst lips
annotate that you were
a cannibal in a past life
*
recline with hand
stretched open
globe of mercury
balances i wake in my
birthday room visions of
dusk petals soon found
buried in the laundry
cupboard my teeth
later found in
an ashtray
*
marmalade hip hop plays
because we are alone how
your voice harmonises to
the calamity of dugongs
*
before i go to sleep i lift
a bucket over my fallible
remains i tilt i pour
fire over my
body good night

swan song

i have spent small infinities
calculating whether or not
god is made of paper
*
i wheeze with an ocean in my veins
drowning beneath the plumage
of your golden resurgence
*
swans monitor
the swamp
silent then
a warning
complimented by
sky birds we must
abandon these bodies at dawn
*
on the carpet of no one's grass
my body is folded
as i drink the colour
of his coiled body
i am reminded
if we become inaudible
soft trees will break the fall
*
if this is all that is left
of our apocalypse
why am i still here
*
the fragile cathedral you
lay your head inside at
night bathes its floor
with the salt of bleach
*

patience removes the rings
from my osseous fingers as i
prepare to throw my body
beneath the waterline
*
carrying nightfall in my palms
i begin to remind myself
of your skull's absence
i look on as a lighthouse
begins to burn

fire

if we were burning

locust door   bends and   we are buried

in repair not   much longer is   it damp with sky

water or perhaps   narcotic footprints on   the ceiling we

have been anticipating   the rising sun in   all our splendour good

morning! gold compass   glare seeping under   our winter flesh sit

upon the ash-licked   deck is there smoke   in the sky please

promise me that you   will never inhale   the air again no

we mustn't burn the   couch who has placed   this fire here and

why what are the   weapons we possess: a   box of matches or

a pyrokinetic mind i   recline with kindling it   is the smoke

that seeks to   avenge us under   four dim asbestos

pillars yes barmore's   in flames no

prayers just get   out in time

clothes that have been donated

one week after
the fire i sleep
on carpet still
settling in to
the townhouse we
wake to a closet of
hanger bones this'll fit
my thinning self she lifts
a bag and upturns a village
of cloth rising i begin
to raise a pyramid of
hieroglyphic charity we
can still smell smoke i
will always be grateful

i live with you

they said move
back to annerley
avondale avenue do
you have fire in your
bathtub grieve
in water you
whisper something
about a phobia of burning i
remember saying once that the
body cannot be solved then i
begin to question where do
the houses go when we
are not home there are
plenty of chances though
we did not take them you're
missing but still our ghost
hovers against the roof keep
your thoughts and scratch
away at the paint all
hours lamp
off lay awake

princess alexandra hospital
or, how to convince myself to stop doing bad things

and as of today i will
metamorphose
eyes to myself
i vow to do so
scraping at all the dust
beneath my better fingernails
quiet like violence
night after night it's the flamingos i
swear another weight on my own
pebbles
down my throat
unlike whales in float nearby
or perhaps monkey debris
could substantiate the difference between
how
in many different ways
i have found a way to return
back to my own body now
maybe it's just sobriety commemorated
with the thought of tampered milk tops
maybe i just became lost or
somehow managed to find cleaning the
house therapeutic in any kind of way
i think yeah that's when you know
shadowed
that's what i meant to say
another week on my own
but i think you just need to
hold your own hand sometimes
that is the only way
you'll get to know yourself
or by tasting lemon juice
how it sears through the flesh
of your tongue

carry

my psychologist says that
i am unbreakable light
says i cannot survive
with my teeth gritted i
say i am made of kinetic
energy and that i am turning
into a blue carrie bradshaw
say that there is a skyscraper
concealed in my wardrobe
black tea bags in the sink
dining room tables carved
into abhorrent shapes say
that there is an artificial shark
tank installed in the bathroom
mirror say that my brain is
made of soggy weet-bix and
that i am not the milk say
that one day i will not be
afraid of barbecues or the
colour of moths worrying
across the wall say that i
have gradually become a citrus
vampire in this very room my
psychologist tells me that
i am not a vampire and
commands me to weep
frequently so i haven't
been back since october

nightmares or, side effects may include

i dream a lot

i dream of a man wandering in a forest
smoke exiting his shoulder blades

i become paint
camouflaged as my skin

i move like rain
and swallow moonlight for dinner

when day comes
i hide beneath
a blanket of air

the man returns to me
moments before i wake

he tells me that water is coming
says it will fill me up heavy
with murky gold
says it will put out the fire

the water becomes an orbed spectrum
escaping the woodland of my pillowcase

lemonade begins
to shut down my organs

in my dream
mexico becomes heaven
for women carrying fire
opals in their coat pockets

last night
suburban dogs find solace
in a meth addict's backyard

goldfinches get married in a tree
then fall to their death
i get a tattoo of it

or machine guns follow me home
until i feed them with haloed water

tonight i bathe with
mermaids in a moss pool
eclipsed around my thighs

without blinking
my collection of spiders
crawl behind my eyeballs

some things
i cannot explain

memory

beep smoke alarm the
house is on fire i think

of how animals
respond to flames

the ways their bodies
bend and twist in glow

charred and you never
really forget don't get

too carried away the
house is warming up

walls echo with scorch
opera then you escape

run and hyperventilate
on wintered ground or

a few months later i lay
on spring grass listening

to music because i like to
drown out the sound of

pale insects trying to tell me
how things went so wrong i

think of eating fire hold
it in my hands and taste

its dissolve on my
tongue or i become

dependent i think
of fire again

bushfire season

distanced smoke and here it is, my opened body. there are triggers for my paradise, my teeth somewhat gaped as i contemplate cold dinners. i can be stagnant as a burn smooths over my already surfaced tongue, or you can help out by disappearing from the country—only for a holiday. it is summertime in the way that my vacationed memory becomes less dim, somewhat transparent. i prefer to sit outside in the exhalation of morning, bird sounds delicately vanishing. there was ash in my coffee yesterday. the horses have been set free in cooroibah. wind shapeshifts into flame and we are all on fire. believe in the water of your mistaken life as you swim your skin through it, oxygen withdrawn from your beloved mouth. we are all crying now.

wisdom teeth

every tooth in my mouth
was once a dinosaur and you
disagree say that things were
difficult last year and now
the leaves are black i have
three eyes and my mouth
is full of wisdom

you, your light

i dreamt there were fireworks last night
reminded me of how
you are cathedral or
i am grace in sandstones
because i know
how to breathe like lanterns
do and why
i am becoming bats
sedated
i am drought
my skin
mirage
or then you are forest
enveloped with wind
or i am the morning of you
we are like driftwood
here is mouth
open
if the coastlines
our bodies endure
beg for water
my hands sense
your lungs
mine
expanding
like the sound a house makes
after burning itself to death
ambience
and know
this is how we evolve

Notes

Earlier versions of these poems first appeared in *Cordite Poetry Review, Australian Poetry Anthology, Plumwood Mountain, Hecate: An Interdisciplinary Journal of Women's Liberation, Rabbit: A Journal for Nonfiction Poetry, Impossible Archetype, Concrescence Zine,* and *Ibis House.*

An earlier version of the poem 'when i tell you to run, you must run' was first published in the chapbook, *Tell Me Like You Mean It: Volume 4* (*Australian Poetry* and *Cordite*, edited by Susie Anderson 2020).

An earlier version of the poem 'house of perpetuating water' was commissioned as a spoken word piece for the Emerging Writers' Festival 2019.

Some fragments that appear in the poem 'supermoon king tides, noosa heads' were taken from my poem 'my night with the necromancer', first published in *Hecate: An Interdisciplinary Journal of Women's Liberation.*

The title of the poem 'venus as a boy in a dream' was taken from the song titled 'Venus as a Boy' performed by Björk.

Acknowledgements

These poems were written on, and inspired by, the stolen lands of the Kabi Kabi/Gubbi Gubbi, Turrbal, and Yuggera people. Sovereignty was never ceded.

I am deeply indebted to Jess Wilkinson, Renee Cahill and the rest of the team at *Rabbit* for all of your blood, sweat and tears, and for believing in this book when I did not, as well as for putting up with me changing everything every five minutes.

Sincerest thanks to Bonny Cassidy for taking the time to read my work and for sharing your words about it.

Thank you, the reader, for holding this book in your hands.

My upmost gratitude to Rory Green for reading an earlier version of this collection, as well as to Melody Paloma, Cham Zhi Yi and the rest of the Toolkittens for providing feedback for earlier drafts of some of these poems all those years back.

Thank you to Connor for always being so supportive and reading through my work. This book wouldn't have been possible without your love, nurturing and incredible advice.

Lastly, but certainly not least, I'm also deeply indebted to my family and my late grandmother Barbara Cave for helping me fall in love with literature and writing. This book wouldn't exist without them.

Rabbit. | *Poets Series*

Mitch Cave's *how to eat fire and why* is published by **Rabbit Poetry Journal** as part of its Rabbit Poets Series.

Rabbit Poetry Journal is a journal for nonfiction poetry, based in Melbourne, Australia. A pioneer in the field, *Rabbit* intends to celebrate the potential for poetry to explore and interrogate the boundaries of nonfiction writing. *Rabbit* encourages poets to openly engage with auto/biography, history, politics, economics, mathematics, cultural analysis, science, the environment, and all other aspects of real world experience, recollection and interpretation.

The Rabbit Poets Series intends to support and promote small single-authored collections of poems by new poets that represent a more extended engagement with the journal's nonfiction framework.

For more information on **Rabbit Poetry Journal** or the Rabbit Poets Series, please visit www.rabbitpoetry.com